Gluten Free Cookbook 2023

1200 Days of Flavorful, Safe and Gluten-Free Innovative Recipes for Those Who Are Intolerant but Still Want Satisfying Meals Through Never-Before-Tried Recipes

Alyson Bennett

Table Of contents

Introduction

As the popularity of gluten-free diets has grown over the last few years, more and more individuals are making the conscious decision to include gluten-free foods and dishes in their regular meals.

Gluten is a kind of protein found in many cereals. Some examples of these grains include wheat, barley, and rye. Celiac disease patients are more prone to have an immunological response to gluten than the general population. Damage to the small intestinal lining might result from this response. This may cause a variety of unpleasant side effects, such as gas, diarrhoea, and stomach pain. Serious health problems including anaemia, osteoporosis, and infertility may develop as a consequence. comparable to celiac disease, but without the immune response and small intestinal damage, non-celiac gluten sensitivity causes symptoms that are comparable to those of celiac disease. Although the exact source of non-celiac gluten sensitivity is unknown, it is thought to originate from an immune reaction to gluten or to one of the other proteins found in wheat, barley, and rye. Despite the fact that the exact cause of this ailment is unknown, some nevertheless hold to this theory.

People with celiac disease or gluten sensitivity that is not due to celiac disease must follow a gluten-free diet to adequately manage symptoms and avoid further damage to the small intestine. Whether or not they have celiac disease, this is the situation. To achieve this goal, you must eliminate all sources of gluten from your diet. Breads, pasta, cereal, and a significant amount of processed meals fall into this category. Gluten may be present in many common foods that are part of a typical Western diet. Because of the abundance of gluten in these products, sticking to a gluten-free diet may be difficult. Gluten-free eaters who are concerned about obtaining enough essential nutrients into their diets should pay close attention to food labels and seek advice from a nutritionist or other healthcare professional. Without this knowledge, people can't be sure they'll be able to maintain their healthy diet.

Avoiding gluten is beneficial not just for those with celiac disease or a gluten sensitivity unrelated to the illness, but also for those who don't have either of those conditions but nevertheless want to improve their digestive health or lose weight. People in this group are not aware that they have celiac disease. There is presently insufficient proof to support the use of a gluten-free diet for general health or weight reduction; however, there is some evidence that following a gluten-free diet may be beneficial for some conditions, such as irritable bowel syndrome (IBS). This is the case even though there is some data suggesting that a gluten-free diet may be helpful for some conditions.

Making sure you're getting enough of the right nutrients might be difficult when you're following a gluten-free diet. Natural gluten-free meals, such fruits, vegetables, and meats, tend to be nutrient-dense and may provide more than one kind of vitamin or mineral. Meats, vegetables, and other foods fall under this category. However, certain gluten-free manufactured foods may have less nutritional value than their gluten-containing counterparts. It's also possible that people on gluten-free diets won't get enough of certain key nutrients like fibre and iron. Those on a gluten-free diet need to be more vigilant about fulfilling their nutritional needs, and may want to see a dietician or supplement their diet with vitamins and minerals to make up for what they're missing.

One of the possible downsides of adhering to a gluten-free diet is an increase in the likelihood of social isolation. Because many eateries and events do not provide gluten-free food alternatives, those on gluten-restrictive diets may find it challenging to go out and socialise. This might make it more challenging to maintain such a diet. Individuals on a gluten-free diet may find it difficult to maintain their diet while simultaneously taking part in social activities due to the difficulties presented by the diet. However, many individuals have found methods to adapt their diets to the needs of their social life, and a wider range of gluten-free eating options are now available.

Despite the difficulty of a gluten-free diet, this remains true. In addition, many who adopt a gluten-free diet for reasons other than Celiac disease report an improvement in their general well-being and a surge in energy levels as a result of the dietary changes they've made. This occurs because to a protein called gluten, which is prevalent in wheat and other grains. Although there is no universally applicable approach to nutrition, some with gluten sensitivities may find that adhering to a gluten-free diet is the best option for their health.

People with gluten-related diseases or digestive troubles may also benefit from trying out some of the other dietary approaches that are available today, in addition to being gluten-free. Irritable Bowel Syndrome (IBS) patients, for example, may find symptom alleviation by following a low-FODMAP diet, which restricts their intake of certain types of carbohydrates that are notoriously difficult to digest. However, it is essential to speak with a healthcare provider or an experienced nutritionist to establish which dietary plan would be the most efficient in addressing the needs of the individual in issue.

Gluten Free Fundamentals

There is no evidence to support the consumption of a gluten-free diet for either general wellbeing or weight reduction, however some individuals choose to do so for reasons such as better digestive health or weight loss. Isolation may increase if following a gluten-free diet prevents you from taking part in extracurricular activities or missing out on social gatherings. Those who become gluten-free for reasons other than celiac disease or gluten sensitivity typically see positive changes in their health and energy levels.

Keep in mind that not all foods without gluten are made equal. Some gluten-free meals are made with whole foods and have a high nutritional density, while others are made with highly processed ingredients and contain few or none. Those on a gluten-free diet should focus on meeting their nutritional requirements via the consumption of whole foods wherever feasible and closely track their food intake.

The Obvious Benefits of Going Gluten-Free

While becoming gluten-free may have some positive side effects, there is no evidence that doing so would improve your health or lead to considerable weight reduction. Here we'll discuss the potential health advantages of eliminating gluten from your diet, including the alleviation of symptoms for individuals who suffer from gluten intolerance, increased vitality and general wellness for some, and relief from the signs and symptoms of certain gastrointestinal disorders.

Improvement in the quality of life for those with gluten-related disorders.

People with celiac disease or non-celiac gluten sensitivity may discover that eliminating gluten from their diet improves digestive health by decreasing gastrointestinal symptoms such gas, bloating, and diarrhoea. It may also prevent further harm to the small intestine and reduce the risk of long-term effects including osteoporosis and anaemia.

A boost in energy and overall happiness for those who experience it

Some people who follow a gluten-free diet claim to have greater stamina and fewer stomach problems as a result. Some persons on a gluten-free diet claim to have improved health as a result, but the data is anecdotal at best. This might be because of differences in how their bodies respond to gluten, or it could be because they are consuming more natural foods and less processed foods. It's important to remember that not everyone will have the same reaction to a gluten-free diet, and that not everyone who eats gluten-free will experience these benefits.

Those with digestive issues, such as Irritable Bowel Syndrome (IBS), may benefit from this.

Some studies have shown that eliminating gluten from the diet may alleviate IBS symptoms for some people with the condition. However, there is conflicting data, and a gluten-free diet may not be appropriate or useful for all people with irritable bowel syndrome (IBS). Working with a registered dietitian or other healthcare professional to determine the optimal dietary approach is crucial.

Details about the diet

Paying close attention to the types of meals selected, the chemicals included in those foods, and the amounts of nutrients provided by those foods is essential while following a gluten-free diet.

We can get fresh stuff.

A healthy diet may include these gluten-free items by nature:

11

- Fruits and vegetables
- Foods that have not been altered in any way, such as raw nuts, seeds, beans, and legumes.
- Eggs
- The bulk of low-fat dairy products Lean cuts of unprocessed red meat, fish, and poultry

The following grains, starches, and flours do not contain gluten and are examples of those that do.

- Rice flour, soy flour, maize flour, potato flour and bean flour are all examples of gluten-free flours.
- Rice, corn, oats, rye, buckwheat, rye berries, rye berries, oat berries,
- There is a complete ban on the following grains: sorghum, cassava-based tapioca (soy), and teff.
- Avoid consuming the following when eating and drinking:

What You'll Need:

- Triticale, a cross between wheat and rye, is cultivated on a commercial scale in addition to barley and wheat.

oats

Oats do not naturally contain gluten, although they may get cross-contaminated with wheat, barley, or rye during processing. Products made with oats and advertised as gluten-free have not been tainted by contact with wheat. However, some people with celiac disease are allergic to oats, even if they are labelled as gluten-free.

Names for various forms of wheat flour reflect variations in the milling process or the manufacturing method. Possible sources of gluten in the following flours:

- Vitamin- and mineral-enriched wheat flour
- Milled wheat, often known as farina, is a prominent ingredient in warm morning cereals.
- Graham flour is a coarse, whole wheat flour used in baking.

- No extra leavening is needed for phosphate flour, often known as no-knead flour.
- The major component of both couscous and pasta is semolina, a residue of wheat processing.

Gluten-free product labels

Before buying a product, check the label to see whether it contains gluten. Any product containing wheat, barley, rye, or triticale, or anything derived from these grains, must identify the grain by name in the list of ingredients. The same is true for every byproduct produced from the grain.

Natural foods that do not include gluten

- A gluten-free, ready-to-eat food item that does not include any gluten-containing components.
- Products that have not been tainted by the presence of gluten-containing substances during processing.
- Foods that formerly contained gluten but have been processed to remove it completely.
- It is possible to label alcoholic drinks as "gluten-free" if they are made using ingredients that do not naturally contain gluten, such as grapes or juniper berries.

Beverages distilled from wheat, barley, rye, or a hybrid grain like triticale may legally claim on their labels that they have been "processed," "treated," or "crafted" to eliminate gluten. However, the label must indicate that the gluten concentration is unknown and that the beverage may contain gluten. These beverages may not be marked as gluten-free even if they are.

Most packaged goods include gluten.

Not only can wheat, barley, and rye exist in a broad variety of foods, but you may also find them in a lot of other things. Thickening, binding, flavouring, or colouring the mixture using wheat or wheat gluten is also possible. Food labels should be checked to ensure that they do not include wheat, barley, or rye.

Unless otherwise specified on the label or prepared using maize, rice, soy or another non-gluten-containing grain, you should not eat the following:

- There is a selection of beers, ales, porters, and stouts. barley is a common ingredient
- Breads
- You'll find crackers, biscuits, candies, cereals, the communion wafers, and a variety of sweet baked items made from bulgur wheat.
- You may use meat and fish gravy with croutons and French fries and vice versa.
- Barley-based goods, including malt and malt flavour.
- Lunchtime fare includes matzo, pasta, and cold cuts and deli meats.
- The wheat-based ingredients in soy sauce and other sauces.
- Rice dishes with a variety of spices
- Tortilla chips, potato chips, and other seasoned snacks.
- Chicken and other fowl that has not been basted.
- Vitamin and medication substitutes Beef broth Canned soups Instant soup mixes Sauced veggies

Getting started with gluten free kitchen

Those who have made the choice to eliminate gluten from their diet may encounter difficulties, especially when they first begin cooking for themselves. It might be confusing to figure out what foods are acceptable and which ones you should avoid since many common ones, like wheat flour, are not permitted. But with little forethought and effort, you can cook gluten-free meals that are not only tasty, but also packed with nutrients. This may be achieved in the kitchen by preparing meals using gluten-free components.

First, learn what kinds of food are healthy and what kinds aren't.

Learning what foods are safe to consume and which ones are off-limits is crucial for anybody beginning a gluten-free diet. Although it may seem like a lot of extra work at first, remember that there are plenty of delicious and healthful gluten-free choices out there. Remembering that this option exists is crucial. Gluten-free grains and flours include rice, quinoa, maize, potato, almond, and coconut, all of which are safe for human consumption. Buckwheat, amaranth, and sorghum are some other grains and flours that don't contain gluten. However, it is crucial to be mindful that soy sauce, salad dressings, and even certain types of vitamins and supplements may be sneaky sources of gluten. To determine whether or not a product contains gluten, one should always read the label carefully before ingesting it.

Use only gluten-free items to stock your kitchen.

Now that you know what you may eat and what you should avoid, you can begin filling your kitchen with gluten-free goods and getting back to normal eating. Gluten-free flours, pasta, bread, oats, and baking powder are some of the most important gluten-free ingredients. In order to add taste to the food you are making, it is essential to have a broad selection of herbs and spices on available. You'll have more leeway to choose from as a result. Buying some gluten-free cookbooks or consulting some gluten-free resources online might be a good option if you're in need of some new ideas for gluten-free dishes. If any of them appeals to you, you have a choice.

Third, put money into high-quality tools made specifically for cooking.

For those who follow a gluten-free diet, it's crucial to stock their kitchens with specialised equipment. A separate set of dishes, utensils and cooking utensils designed specifically for gluten-free cooking. You may also consider purchasing a dedicated gluten-free bread toaster, since standard toasters can easily contaminate gluten-free bread with crumbs from regular bread.

Fourth, plan your meals ahead of time.

Meal preparation is an important part of any healthy diet, but it is especially crucial for those following a gluten-free diet. If you plan your meals in advance, you can avoid last-minute trips to the shop and ensure you always have gluten-free options on hand. Invest some time every week to plan your meals and snacks, and compile a shopping list based on your plans. You may be certain that you will always have access to healthy, gluten-free food and that tension won't have a chance to set in.

Experiment with New Ingredients and Recipes in Your Kitchen

You shouldn't be afraid to experiment often in your gluten-free kitchen with different recipes and ingredients. Trying out new things is a great way to keep your meals fresh

16

and enjoyable and there are many delicious dishes that do not involve gluten that you may explore. Think about trying quinoa or millet, two gluten-free grains, or making your own gluten-free bread or pasta. It's possible you'll discover a new favourite food that you would have avoided otherwise.

By using these guidelines for setting up a gluten-free kitchen, you can ensure that you always have access to delicious and nutritious gluten-free meals and snacks. If you put in the time and effort ahead of time, switching to a gluten-free diet might be a simple and enjoyable process.

"Breakfast

1. French Omelet

Ingredients

1. ¼ tsp.salt
2. 1/8 of a tsp.of ground black pepper
3. Butter equivalent to 2 Tbs

Steps To Cook:

1. Eggs, salt, and pepper should be mixed together in a basin. Using a fork, blend the ingredients until there are no white threads remaining, but do not beat them until they become foamy.
2. Butter should be melted in a pan with flared sides that is 8 inches in diameter and nonstick. After the foaming of the butter has stopped, add the egg. Shake the pan in a back-and-forth motion with one hand while continuously stirring the ingredients with the other using a fork. A delicate and smooth curd is produced by the fork tines. Use chopsticks or bamboo skewers if you are afraid about scratching your skin when using your skilled.

3. Continue to shake and mix the eggs, scraping the sides of the bowl regularly, until the eggs are set but still have a little bit of moisture in them. You may crumble some cheese over the top at this stage if you want.

4. To tilt the pan, bring your hand with the palm facing up beneath the handle of the pan, and then tilt the pan to an angle of roughly 45 degrees. Fold one-third of the omelet over into itself using a spatula, then repeat with the other third of the omelet.

5. The omelet should be flipped over so that it falls with the seam down when the skillet is inverted over a dish. Makes 1 serving.

2. Quinoa and peanut butter

Ingredients

1. 2 ounces of water
2. 1 Cups quinoa
3. ¼ Cups apple juice or cider
4. 3 Tbsof reduced-fat creamy peanut butter
5. 1 small banana, cut into chunks
6. 2 Tbs of spreadable fruit, preferably raspberry or strawberry
7. 4 milligrams of peanuts that have been blanched but not salted

Steps To Cook:

1. "Give the quinoa and water a thorough toss in a saucepan of enough size to combine the two. First, bring the water to a full boil, and then turn it down to medium-low after it's boiling. Cook the rice with the cover on for 10 to 15 minutes, or until all the water is absorbed, depending on how much time you have. Quickly remove the pan from the hob.
2. Stirring constantly, add the apple juice to the saucepan of quinoa until the peanut butter has been well incorporated. Add the mashed banana to the remaining ingredients and mix well.
3. It's important to evenly distribute the ingredients across the four bowls.
4. Distribute the fruit equally among the bowls, using one level tablespoon each serving.
5. Before serving, sprinkle one tablespoon of chopped peanuts over each portion.
6. When you're serving, keep a sense of humour about it.

3. Bacon, Potato, and Kale Frittata

Ingredients

1. 12 ounces of young potatoes with red peel, cut into quarters
2. 6 slices of bacon with a reduced sodium and fat content, roughly chopped
3. 2 Cups of fresh kale, finely chopped
4. ½ Cups of onion that has been roughly diced 8 eggs, beaten just briefly.

Steps To Cook:

1. The potatoes should be cooked for about ten minutes in a medium saucepan that has been covered with a lid and contains water that has been brought to a boil and is lightly salted. Cook the potatoes just until they are ready to eat. Drain, then set to the side.
2. In the meantime, the grill should be preheated. Cook the bacon in a large skillet that has flared sides and can bear direct heat from the grill over medium-high heat until it begins to get crispy. Continue to simmer the mixture for approximately 5 minutes, or until the onion is tender, after adding the kale and the onion. After the potatoes have been boiled, mix in the mashed potatoes.
3. In a medium bowl, eggs, a quarter of a tsp.of salt, and a quarter of a tsp.of ground black pepper should be combined using a whisk. The mixture should then be set aside.
4. Combine the egg mixture with the potato mixture in a bowl. Cook over a heat that is medium-low. Run a spatula along the edge of the pan as the mixture begins to set, raising the egg mixture so that the uncooked part flows below. Keep heating and gently raising the sides until the egg mixture has nearly reached the desired consistency.
5. Put the skillet under the broiler at a distance of between 4 and 5 inches from the flame. For about a minute to a minute and a half in the broiler, or until the top is set and no longer moist. (Alternatively, preheat the oven to 400 degrees Fahrenheit and bake the cake for approximately 5 minutes, or until the top is firm and no longer moist.) Let stand for 5 minutes. Using a spatula, transfer the frittata to a serving plate. Divide into six equal-sized wedges.

4. Gluten Free Banana Bread

Ingredients

1. 5 unpeeled bananas
2. 2 Cups Gluten-Free Flour Mix
3. 1 and a half teaspoons of baking powder that is gluten-free
4. ½ tsp.baking soda
5. ½ tsp.of cinnamon powder
6. ¼ tsp.salt
7. ¼ Tbs Nutmeg
8. 1/8 tsp.of ginger powder
9. 2 eggs, whisked very briefly.
10. 1 Cups sugar
11. ½ Cups vegetable oil or melted butter
12. 1Cups of walnuts chopped

Gluten Free Flour Mix

1. 3 Cups flour made from white rice
2. 3 Cups potato starch
3. 2 measuring Cups of sorghum flour
4. Xanthan gum, equivalent to 4 teaspoons

Steps To Cook:

1. Bring the temperature in the oven up to 350 degrees. Prepare one 9x5x3-inch or two 7 1/2x3 1/2x2-inch loaf pans by greasing the bottoms and the sides for a further half an inch, and then put aside. Prepare a baking tray that is 15 by 10 by 1 inches with foil. Arrange the bananas in the pan that has been coated with foil. Use the tines of a fork to make holes in the banana skin at regular intervals of one inch. Bake for 15 minutes (the peels will turn dark brown). Cool bananas in pan.
2. Mix the Gluten-Free Flour Mix, the baking powder, the baking soda, the cinnamon, the salt, the nutmeg, and the ginger in a large basin. Create a well in the middle of the flour mixture, and put it to the side.

3. Eggs, sugar, and oil should be mixed together in a basin of medium size, then put aside. Use a tiny, sharp knife to split the banana skins, then remove and dispose of the peels. To get 1 1/2 Cups of roasted bananas, measure the pulp of the bananas by pressing them gently into measuring Cups, then add the roasted bananas into the egg mixture. Combine the flour mixture with the egg mixture all at once. Stir just until moistened (batter should be lumpy). Mix with some chopped walnuts. Put the batter into the loaf pan that has been prepared.

4. Bake the 9-inch pan for 55-60 minutes, up to the point that a wooden toothpick inserted in the centre comes out clean; do the same with the 7 1/2-inch pans, but reduce the baking time to 45-55 minutes. Cover with foil in a loose manner for the last 15 minutes of baking if required to avoid the food from being too brown.

5. Five, let the pan cool on a wire rack for ten minutes. Remove from heat. Put your feet up and relax on the wire rack. To get the best results when slicing, wrap it up and let it rest in the fridge overnight. After resting, the quick bread will have a more uniformly moist texture with less crumbliness.

Non-Gluten Flour Blend

1. First, using a whisk and a big, airtight container, combine the rice flour, potato starch, sorghum flour, and xanthan gum.
2. If the jar is sealed, it may be kept for three months at room temperature.
3. Third, when you pull out the toothpick, you could find a few crumbs stuck to it, but there shouldn't be any raw batter clinging to it. The following is advice.

5. Buttermilk Biscuits with Sausage Gravy

Ingredients

1. 3 Cups Gluten-Free Flour Mix*
2. 1 Tbs sugar
3. 1 Tbs gluten-free baking powder
4. 1 tsp.salt
5. 1/3 tsp.of cream of tartar
6. ½ Cups of shortening
7. ¼ Cups butter
8. 1 ¼ Cups buttermilk or 1 Cups milk
9. 2 Tbs butter, melted
10. 1 recipe Gluten-Free Sausage Gravy
11. Fresh chives that have been chopped (optional)

Gluten-Free Sausage Gravy

1. 1 ½ pound bulk pork sausage
2. 1 ounce of finely chopped onion (1 large)
3. ½ Cups of gluten-free flour blend
4. 3 Cups milk
5. Salt with black pepper
6. 2 teaspoons of fresh thyme, pinched in the corner.

Gluten Free Flour Mix

1. 3 Cups flour made from white rice
2. 3 Cups potato starch
3. 2 Cups sorghum flour
4. 4 teaspoons Xanthan gum

Steps To Cook:

1. Prepare the oven to 450 degrees Fahrenheit by turning the temperature dial. It is recommended that the first five components be brought together in a big basin

using a swirling motion to ensure that they are thoroughly combined. (By employing the utilisation of cream of tartar).

2. Reduce the shortening and a quarter cup of the butter with a pastry blender until the flour mixture forms coarse crumbs. This should take around ten minutes. Mix in the remaining butter with the other ingredients. It is essential to make a well in the middle of the flour mixture and place the liquid in there. The entire quantity of buttermilk should be poured into the basin all at once. Use a fork to give the mixture a very quick stir so that it can absorb the liquid.

3. In order to knead the dough, you need first place it on a surface that has been dusted with the additional flour mixture in a very light layer. The dough should be kneaded by folding it and gently pressing it against one another until it comes together. Pat or roll the dough out very gently until it is an inch thick when you reach the desired thickness. Cut shapes out of the dough using a round or square biscuit cutter that has been coated with flour and measures 2 1/2 inches. Between each cut, the cookie cutter should be dunked into the flour mixture, and the scraps should be rerolled as necessary.

4. When you have finished cutting out shapes from the dough, you should spread them out in an even manner on a baking sheet that has not been oiled. Cover with buttered that has been melted, then season with salt and pepper. Bake 15 to 18 minutes or until golden. After removing the item from the oven, set it on a wire rack so that it can cool down more gradually.

5. Split biscuits. When you are ready to serve, pour gluten-free sausage gravy into each individual dish, and if you'd like, you may also sprinkle the tops with chopped chives.

Gluten-Free Sausage Gravy

1. First, in a large pan, over medium heat, brown half a pound of bulk pork sausage and one cup of chopped onion, breaking up the meat with a wooden spoon as it cooks. While it's cooking, add a cup of water.

2. How long you cook an onion for will determine how soft it becomes. Do not drain. One-fourth cup of gluten-free flour is required. Before adding anything to the meat, combine all the ingredients in a dish. Mix into the ground meat.

3. Third, while still whisking, gradually pour in the three cups of milk. Maintain continual stirring until the fluid starts to boil and thickens.

4. Stirring the mixture for a further minute while cooking is step four. Before serving, sprinkle in little salt and pepper to taste. Freshly sliced thyme leaves, about two tablespoons' worth, should be added to the mixture. About 5 Cups of food may be obtained from this recipe.

Non-Gluten Flour Blend

1. First, using a whisk and a big, airtight container, combine the rice flour, potato starch, sorghum flour, and xanthan gum. You may store the jar at room temperature for up to three months as long as you keep the lid on it.

6. Cassava Pancakes

Ingredients

2. ¾ Cups cassava (100% yucca root) flour
3. 1 ½ tsp.baking powder
4. ½ tsp.salt
5. 1/2 Cups of coconut milk from a can, unsweetened
6. 1/4 mug of water
7. 1 egg
8. 2 Tbs. pure maple syrup
9. 1 Tbs olive oil

Steps To Cook:

1. In a medium-sized basin, you should use a whisk to combine the dry ingredients of baking powder, salt, and flour. In a small basin, use a whisk to combine the coconut milk, water, egg, maple syrup, and oil.
2. The mixture should be placed in the basin. Incorporate into the whole mixture of flour. Just until everything is combined, mix the ingredients together.
3. Each pancake should have about a quarter cup of batter poured upon it before it is placed on a hot griddle that has been lightly greased.
4. In cases where it is necessary, distribute the batter. Cook the pancakes for two to three minutes on each side over medium heat, or until they have a golden brown colour all over.
5. When the tops of the pancakes begin to bubble and the edges get a little dry, you should flip them.
6. To be consumed while heated. Just before serving, a little coating of maple syrup should be sprinkled over the dish.

7. Cake Donuts

Ingredients

1. Mixture of gluten-free flour equaling 4 Cups
2. Baking powder that is gluten-free, 2 teaspoons
3. ½ tsp.salt
4. 2 eggs
5. 1 ¼ Cups granulated sugar
6. 1 tsp.gluten-free vanilla
7. ⅔Cups milk
8. ¼ Cups butter, melted
9. Vegetable oil or shortening for deep-fat frying
10. Icing sugar that does not include gluten (optional)

Gluten Free Flour Mix

1. 3 Cups flour made from white rice
2. 3 Cups potato starch
3. 2 Cups sorghum flour
4. 4 teaspoons Xanthan gum

Steps To Cook:

1. In combine the baking powder, salt, and Gluten-Free Flour Mix in a large bowl and stir to combine. To make a thick enough mixture to use, whisk the eggs, sugar, and vanilla extract in a large bowl for three minutes on medium speed. In a bowl with a low rim, combine the milk and melted butter.
2. While continually beating on low speed, add the flour mixture and the milk combination to the egg mixture and fold until just combined. You'll have to add the flour mixture and the milk mixture again. (If necessary, incorporate the remaining flour mixture.) Refrigerate the dough in a plastic bag for at least an hour.
3. Third, scatter the remaining flour mixture over the top of the table or counter. Roll the dough out to a thickness of 1 cm to get halfway there. Donut-shaped slices

were made in the dough using a donut cutter that had been coated with flour. Flour the cutter between each cut, then re-roll the remnants.

4. The oil (which should be between one and two inches thick) should be heated to 365 degrees Fahrenheit in a large, heavy pot. For approximately two minutes total, fry the donuts in two- or three-piece batches, or until brown on both sides. Using a slotted spoon, remove the food from the pan and let it to drain on paper towels. After a few minutes, sprinkle the donuts with more granulated sugar. (wait till it has cooled before dusting with powdered sugar).

8. Egg Bites Inspired

Ingredients

1. Spray for cooking that doesn't stick
2. 8 eggs
3. 4 pieces of bacon, cooked till crispy and crumbled.
4. ½ Cups of chopped fresh spinach
5. 1/3Cups of chopped roasted red bell peppers
6. 1/2 Cups of shredded Monterey Jack, white cheddar, Gouda, or Gruyere cheese
7. ½ tsp.salt
8. 1/8 tsp.of black pepper in ground form
9. Cream cheese, finely chopped fresh chives
10. Spicy pepper sauce are all great toppings for this dish. (optional)

Steps To Cook:

1. Bring the temperature in the oven up to 325 degrees. Spray six half-pint jars with nonstick cooking spray and place them in a wide-mouthed cabinet. Put the jars in a baking dish that is 13 by 9 by 2 inches.
2. Eggs, bacon, spinach, bell peppers, cheese, salt, and pepper should be mixed together in a large bowl using a whisk. Divide among prepared jars. Put the rack in the oven where the pan with the jars is. Pour enough heated water into the pan so that it comes up the sides of the jars about halfway. Bake 35 to 40 minutes or until eggs are set,
3. Reduce the heat a little. If you'd like, you may finish the dish with crème fraiche, chives, and/or spicy sauce.

9. Zucchini Muffins with Greek Yogurt Icing

Ingredients

1. 1 Cups gluten-free all-purpose flour
2. 1 Cups gluten-free oats
3. ¼ Cups granulated sugar
4. 1/3 Cups of brown sugar, packed
5. 1 level tsp.of cinnamon powder
6. ½ Tbs Baking powder that is gluten-free
7. ½ tsp.salt
8. ¼ tsp.baking soda
9. 2 eggs, whisked very briefly.
10. 1/4 Cups of milk that is fat-free
11. 1 ounce (or Cups) of cooked quinoa*
12. 1 Cups of zucchini that has been roughly shredded
13. 1/2 Cups of apple sauce without added sugar
14. ¼ Cups canola oil
15. 1 tsp.gluten-free vanilla
16. 1 recipe of frosting made with Greek yogurt
17. 1/2 tsp.of lemon peel that has been coarsely shredded

Greek Yogurt Frosting

1. 1 pack of plain, fat-free Greek yogurt measuring 5.3 ounces
2. 3 Tbs of icing sugar powder
3. 1 tsp.vanilla

Steps To Cook:

1. Raise to a temperature of 350 degrees the temperature in the oven. To make a dozen muffin cups with a diameter of 2 1/2 inches, spray them with cooking spray and set them aside while you prepare the rest of the ingredients.
2. In a big basin, a wooden spoon should be utilised to combine the following ingredients: flour, granulated sugar, brown sugar, cinnamon, baking powder, salt

and baking soda. Make a hole in the centre of the flour mixture, and then move it to the side of the bowl.

3. In a bowl of about average size, whisk together the eggs and milk. Stir in quinoa, zucchini, applesauce, oil and vanilla. When you are adding the quinoa mixture to the flour mixture, make sure to add it all at once and whisk the ingredients together very gently. Put batter into the prepared muffin cups, filling each one up to about three-quarters of the way to its maximum capacity.

4. Bake for approximately 25 minutes, or until a wooden toothpick inserted in the centre comes out clean. Give it five minutes to cool in the muffin cups, which should be placed on a wire rack. Remove the muffins from their separate cups and set them aside. Relax on the wire rack to the absolute fullest extent. The tops of the muffins should be covered in Greek Yoghurt Frosting, and lemon peel should be sprinkled over each one right before they are served.

Greek Yoghurt Frosting

1. In a small dish, blend the vanilla essence, powdered sugar, and yoghurt until everything is incorporated. It yields around three quarters of a cup.

2. You can serve these muffins, which are only moderately sweet, with a simple drizzle of honey instead of frosting if you do not wish to use frosting on them.

10. Breakfast Salad with Avocado and Eggs

Ingredients

1. 1/2 Cups of parsley, flat-leaf, packed and measured out
2. 1/2 Cups of fresh basil and/or dill, packed and measured out
3. 1 clove of garlic, cut in half
4. 1 lemon (1/2 tsp. zest, 2 Tbs. juice)
5. 1 small avocado, halved
6. 2 measuring spoons of water
7. 2 Tbs olive oil
8. ¼ tsp.salt
9. 1/4 tsp.of black pepper in ground form
10. 1 big carrot
11. 2 butter head lettuce heads, such as Bibb or Boston, torn into bite-sized pieces (11 Cups)
12. 1/3 Cups of radishes that have been thinly sliced
13. 1 and a half pinches of white vinegar
14. 6 eggs

Steps To Cook:

1. First, chop the parsley, basil, and garlic using a food processor until they are uniform in size and put aside.
2. The ingredients should include half an avocado, the chopped peel and juice of one lemon, olive oil, two cups of water, a quarter teaspoon of crushed black pepper, and a pinch of salt. Combine thoroughly. Enclose it and combine it until it reaches a uniform consistency.
3. The remaining half of the avocado should be finely chopped and left aside. Make long, thin ribbons by peeling the carrot in a longitudinal direction. Get the carrot all scrubbed up. Combine the salad dressing with the lettuce, radishes, avocado, and carrot in a large bowl and toss to combine. Quick service is required for the salad.

4. In a large pot, bring the vinegar and six cups of water to a boil. After the mixture comes to a boil, reduce the heat to a simmer and keep it there. Place the eggs gently one by one into the water. Simmer for a further 3–5 minutes, or until the egg whites are hard and the yolks have thickened. The eggs may be removed from the water using a slotted spoon. When eggs are added to a salad, the flavour really pops. This is enough for six people to eat.

"Lunch

11. Apple Crisp that is Gluten-Free

Ingredients

1. 4 Cups peeled, thinly sliced apples
2. 1 tbs. lemon juice
3. 1/4 Cups sugar.
4. 1/4 Cups of an all-purpose
5. A half-tsp. of ground cinnamon
6. Half a Cups of old-fashioned rolled oats free of gluten
7. Half a Cups of a gluten-free all-purpose flour and oat flour blend
8. One and a half Cups of packaged brown sugar
9. Half a milligrams of ground cinnamon
10. 14 tsp.salt
11. A half Cups of softened unsalted butter

Steps To Cook:

1. First, set the oven temperature to 375 degrees Fahrenheit and have it ready.
2. Make sure your baking dish is 8 inches on a side.

3. Third, cut apples into thin slices and sprinkle with lemon juice to serve as an appetizer.
4. Separate a bowl from the rest of the ingredients and combine the powdered cinnamon, gluten-free all-purpose flour blend, and granulated sugar.
5. Shake the container vigorously after adding the sugar mixture to the apples, so that the sugar is evenly distributed.
6. Sixth, when the baking dish has been prepared, pour in the apple mixture.
7. Mix the gluten-free all-purpose flour blend, brown sugar, cinnamon, and salt with the gluten-free rolled oats in a separate dish.
8. Work the melted unsalted butter into the dry ingredients with a pastry cutter or your hands until you have a coarse texture.
9. Cover the apples entirely with the oat mixture in the baking dish.
10. Cook in a 350F oven for 35-40 minutes, or until the apples are soft and the topping is golden. The topping should have reached a golden brown color by now.
11. Allow the apple crisp to cool for 10 minutes after taking it out of the oven.

12. Baked Ziti

Ingredients Needed:

2. 1 packet gluten-free ziti pasta (such as Barilla)
3. 1 pound ground beef
4. 1 medium onion, chopped 2 garlic cloves, peeled and minced
5. 1 can of tomatoes in smashed form
6. 1 can tomato sauce
7. 1 tsp. dried basil
8. 1 tsp. dried oregano
9. To taste, salt and pepper
10. 1 Cups ricotta cheese
11. 1 egg
12. 2 Cups shredded mozzarella cheese

Steps To Cook: To Cook:

1. First, cook the gluten-free ziti according the package's directions.
2. Two, cook the ground beef in a big pan over moderate heat.
3. Third, put the garlic and onion in the pan and cook them over medium heat for three minutes, or until the onion is tender.
4. Combine the crushed tomatoes, tomato sauce, dry oregano, and dry basil in a large basin.
5. Adjust the salt and pepper to your liking (5). This phase might take anywhere from 16-20 minutes of low simmering, depending on the desired sauce thickness.
6. Using two separate bowls, beat one egg, and then incorporate it into the ricotta.
7. After step 8 is complete, preheat the oven to 375 degrees Fahrenheit.
8. After the ziti has been cooked, step eight involves mixing in the meat sauce.
9. Into a 9-by-13-inch baking dish, place half of the spaghetti mixture.
10. Globs of the ricotta cheese mixture should be spooned over the spaghetti.
11. Scatter some shredded mozzarella cheese over the twelve.
12. Don't stop piling until you can no longer make out the individual components in your dish.

13. Place the dish in a warm oven for 30-35 minutes with the foil covering it, or until the cheese is melted and bubbling.
14. Remove the foil and bake for a further 5-10 minutes if you like a golden brown top.
15. Let the cooked ziti sit for five minutes to cool down before serving.

13. Beef Stroganoff

Ingredients

2. 1 pound of sirloin steak, cut very thinly
3. 2 Tbs. Olive oil
4. 1 onion, diced
5. 2 garlic cloves, chopped or minced
6. 1 ounce of sliced mushrooms and 1 Cups
7. 1 ounce of beef stock
8. 1 Cups sour cream
9. 1 Tbs of Worcestershire sauce that does not contain gluten
10. 1 level tsp.of cornstarch
11. To taste, salt and pepper is available.
12. Gluten-free egg noodles

Steps To Cook:

1. In a large saucepan, heat the olive oil over medium heat.
2. The second step is to add the sirloin steak, thinly sliced, once the meat has browned and continue to sauté for another two or three minutes.
3. The third step is to remove the steak from the pan and place it on a serving plate near to the stove.
4. After two or three minutes of sautéing, the onion and garlic may be added since they will be soft enough to be incorporated into the meal.
5. Until they are to your taste, sauté the mushroom slices for two to three minutes.
6. Step 6 calls for bringing the beef broth addition to a boil in the same pot it was cooked in during step 5.
7. In a small bowl, combine the sour cream, gluten-free Worcestershire sauce, corn flour, and spices of your choosing.
8. After adding the sour cream mixture, shake the dish well to distribute the ingredients evenly.
9. After browning the steak on both sides, put it back in the pan and lower the heat to a simmer. The ideal cooking time for a steak is ten to fifteen minutes at a low simmer, depending on the thickness of the sauce and how well done you want it.

10. While the remainder of the dinner is being cooked, make the gluten-free egg noodles according to the package's directions.
11. Serve the beef stroganoff over the heated spaghetti after the noodles are done cooking.

14. Tacos

Ingredients

1. 1 pound ground beef
2. 1 Tbs. vegetable oil
3. 1 onion, diced
4. 2 garlic cloves, chopped or minced
5. 1 milligram of chili powder
6. 1/2 milligram of ground cumin
7. To taste, salt and pepper is available.
8. Shells for tacos that are free of gluten
9. Shredded lettuce
10. Tomatoes cut into cubes Shredded cheddar cheese
11. Cream fraiche

Steps To Cook:

1. Bring the vegetable oil to a simmer over a medium temperature in a large pan. After adding the onion and garlic, give the combination a rapid sauté for about two to three minutes, or until the onion is more soft.
2. After adding the ground beef, continue to sauté it while breaking it up with a spoon until it looks browned and is cooked all the way through.
3. Toss the ingredients after you've added the chilli powder and cumin powder to make sure they're well distributed.
4. Salt and pepper may be used as seasonings on the cuisine.
5. The gluten-free taco shells must be cooked in accordance with the directions, which state whether to do it in the oven or the microwave.
6. When the beef mixture is done cooking, serve it by placing a portion in each taco shell.
7. Top the nachos with a little amount of sour cream, followed by lettuce, tomato, cheddar cheese, and chopped lettuce."

15. "Fried Rice

Ingredients

1. 3 Cups of white rice that has been cooked (preferably day-old)
2. 2 Tbs. vegetable oil
3. 1 onion, diced
4. 2 garlic cloves, chopped or minced
5. 1 Cups chopped carrots
6. 1 Cups frozen peas
7. 3 eggs, whisked very briefly.
8. 3 Tbs of soy sauce that is free of gluten
9. To taste, salt and pepper is available.

Steps To Cook:

1. Start by preheating a large pan or wok over high heat for only a few minutes to get the vegetable oil ready to use.
2. After a minute or so of stirring, you may add the onion and garlic and continue cooking.
3. Carrots may be made fork-tender in a stir-fry in about three to four minutes.
4. Frozen peas should be added to the skillet and stir-fried for a further minute or two, or until they are no longer hard from being frozen.
5. Fifth, push the vegetables to one side of the skillet or wok, and last, pour the beaten eggs into the empty side.
6. The sixth stage, after the eggs have been beaten and cooked, is to add the vegetables. The eggs must first be scrambled.
7. After the white rice has been cooked, toss it into a hot frying pan or wok and stir-fry for two to three minutes.
8. Season with salt and pepper to taste, then stir in the gluten-free soy sauce.

16. Shepherd's Pie

Ingredients

1. 2 Tbs. Olive oil
2. 1 onion, diced
3. 2 garlic cloves, chopped or minced
4. 1 pound ground beef
5. 2 Cups frozen mixed veggies (such as peas, carrots, and corn)
6. 1 ounce of beef stock
7. 2 Tbs tomato paste
8. 1 tsp dried thyme
9. To taste, salt and pepper is available.
10. 3 Cups of mashed potatoes
11. 1/3 Cups of milk
12. 2Tbs of butter.

Steps To Cook:

1. First, preheat the oven to 375 degrees F.
2. Second, heat the olive oil in a large pan over medium heat.
3. The onion and garlic should be added and sautéed for approximately three minutes, or until the onion is tender.
4. Fourth, after the ground beef has been added, it should be cooked thoroughly by sautéing it while breaking it up with a spatula until it is browned.
5. After step 4, add the frozen vegetables, beef broth, tomato paste, dry thyme, salt, and pepper.
6. Maintain a low simmer for 10 to 15 minutes, or until the liquid has thickened somewhat.
7. Pour the meat mixture into a 9x13-inch baking dish and spread it out evenly.
8. Spread a thin layer of mashed potatoes over the meat mixture.
9. After preheating the oven to 400 degrees, place the potatoes inside and bake for 20 to 25 minutes, or until they are golden brown.
10. After the shepherd's pie has cooled for ten minutes, you may serve it.

17. Chicken Pot Pie

Ingredients Needed:

1. 2 Cups of gluten-free flour mix suitable for all purposes (such as King Arthur)
2. 1/2 tsp. salt
3. 1/2 milliliter of xanthan gum
4. 2/3 Cups cold unsalted butter, sliced into tiny cubes
5. 1 egg
6. 3 to 4 Tbs of cold water

With regard to the filling:

1. 2 Tbs. unsalted butter
2. 1 onion, diced
3. 2 garlic cloves, chopped or minced
4. 2 Cups of diced chicken that has been cooked.
5. 2 Cups frozen mixed veggies
6. 2 measures of chicken stock
7. 1 Cups milk
8. 1/4 Cups of a gluten-free combination of all-purpose and specialty flours
9. 1 tsp. dried thyme
10. To taste, salt and pepper

Steps To Cook: To Cook:

1. First, preheat the oven to 375 degrees F.
2. Second, heat the olive oil in a large pan over medium heat.
3. The onion and garlic should be added and sautéed for approximately three minutes, or until the onion is tender.
4. Fourth, after the ground beef has been added, it should be cooked thoroughly by sautéing it while breaking it up with a spatula until it is browned.
5. After step 4, add the frozen vegetables, beef broth, tomato paste, dry thyme, salt, and pepper.
6. Maintain a low simmer for 10 to 15 minutes, or until the liquid has thickened somewhat.

44

7. Pour the meat mixture into a 9x13-inch baking dish and spread it out evenly.
8. Spread a thin layer of mashed potatoes over the meat mixture.
9. After preheating the oven to 400 degrees, place the potatoes inside and bake for 20 to 25 minutes, or until they are golden brown.
10. After the shepherd's pie has cooled for ten minutes, you may serve it..

18. Cookies filled with chocolate chips

Ingredients Needed:

1. 1/2 Cups unsalted butter, softened
2. 1/2 Cups granulated sugar
3. ½ Cups of dark brown sugar
4. 1 egg
5. 1 tsp vanilla extract
6. 1 Cups of gluten-free flour mix suitable for all purposes
7. 1/2 tsp baking powder
8. 1/2 tsp baking soda
9. 1/2 tsp salt
10. 1 Cups of chocolate chips that are gluten-free

Steps To Cook: To Cook:

1. First, get the oven ready at 375 degrees F.
2. Second, prepare a baking sheet by covering it with parchment paper.
3. Third, make the frosting by beating the softened butter, granulated sugar, and brown sugar together in a large mixer until frothy.
4. In a separate dish, whisk together the egg and vanilla essence.
5. Mix the gluten-free all-purpose flour blend, baking powder, baking soda, and salt in a separate bowl from the other ingredients.
6. Sixth, while constantly stirring, gradually add the dry ingredients to the butter mixture.
7. Seventh, mix in some gluten-free chocolate chips.
8. Separate the dough balls by approximately 2 inches on the prepared baking sheet and drop them in by the tablespoonful.
9. Cook for 10-12 minutes in a preheated oven.
10. Wait 5 minutes after removing the cookies from the oven before moving them to a wire rack to finish cooling.

19. Lasagna

Ingredients Needed:

1. 1 packet gluten-free lasagna noodles (such as Tinkyada)
2. 1 pound ground beef
3. 1 medium onion, chopped 2 garlic cloves, peeled and minced
4. 1 can diced tomatoes
5. 1 can tomato sauce
6. 1 Tbs dried basil
7. 1 tsp dried oregano
8. To taste, salt and pepper is available.
9. 1 Cups ricotta cheese
10. 1 egg
11. 2 Cups shredded mozzarella cheese

Steps To Cook:

1. First, make the gluten-free lasagna noodles according the instructions on the package.
2. To begin, cook the ground beef in a large skillet over medium heat.
3. The onion and garlic should be added and sautéed for approximately three minutes, or until the onion is tender.
4. Put in the dried oregano and basil, along the chopped tomatoes and tomato sauce.
5. Season with salt and pepper to taste. 5.
6. Sixteen to twenty minutes, depending on how thick you want your sauce, at a low simmer should do it.
7. Seven, in separate bowls, mix together 1 egg and 1 cup of ricotta cheese.
8. Set the oven temperature to 375 degrees F.
9. To make the lasagna, stack prepared gluten-free lasagna noodles in a 9-by-13-inch baking dish.
10. Ten. Using a spoon, evenly coat the noodles with the beef sauce.
11. Spoon some of the ricotta cheese mixture on top of the beef sauce.
12. Shredded mozzarella cheese should be put on top.
13. Keep stacking until there is nothing left in the dish.

14. Bake, covered with foil, for 30 to 35 minutes, or until the cheese is melted and bubbling, in an oven preheated to the correct temperature.
15. Remove the foil and bake for 5-10 more minutes, or until the top is golden brown.
16. When the lasagna has cooled, wait five minutes before cutting it.

20. Gluten-Free Banana Bread

Ingredients Needed:

1. 2 Cups of a gluten-free all-purpose flour mix (like Bob's Red Mill),
2. 1 tsp baking soda
3. 1/4 tsp salt
4. 1/2 Cups unsalted butter, softened
5. 3/4 of a Cups of dark brown sugar
6. 2 eggs
7. 3 ripe bananas, mashed
8. 1/2 Cups of walnuts that have been chopped (optional)

Steps To Cook: To Cook:

1. Step one: set the oven temperature to a scorching 350 degrees Fahrenheit.
2. Spray a loaf pan that measures 9 by 5 inches with cooking spray.
3. Third, mix the baking soda, salt, and gluten-free all-purpose flour in a large basin.
4. Fourth, whip the softened butter and granulated sugar together in a separate dish until light and creamy.
5. Five, after pounding, add the mashed bananas and eggs.
6. Stirring constantly at step six, add the dry ingredients to the banana mixture gradually.
7. Seven, if you're using chopped walnuts, add those now.
8. Pour the batter into the ready loaf pan.
9. Put in a preheated oven for 50-60 minutes, or until a toothpick inserted in the middle of the loaf comes out clean.
10. After letting the banana bread rest for ten minutes in the pan, turn it out onto a wire rack to cool fully.

21. Chicken prepared on a grill

Ingredients Needed:

1. 4 chicken breasts that have been removed of the bones and skin.
2. 2 Tbs olive oil
3. 2 garlic cloves, chopped or minced
4. 1 tsp dried thyme
5. To taste, salt and pepper is available.

Steps To Cook

1. Preheat the grill or grpan to a high temperature, perhaps in the middle of medium and high.
2. Mix the olive oil, garlic, and thyme in a bowl or basin with a shallow rim using a whisk.
3. Before starting the cooking process, season the chicken breasts with salt and pepper to taste before adding them for the frying pan.
4. Use the olive oil and garlic combination as a garnish for the chicken.
5. Grill the chicken for 6-7 minutes each side, or until an instant-read thermometer registers 165 degrees F.
6. Wait five minutes after removing the chicken from the oven before slicing and serving.

22. Gluten-Free Mac and Cheese

Ingredients Needed:

1. 1 packet of elbow macaroni that is free of gluten (such as Barilla)
2. 4 Tbs. unsalted butter
3. 4 Tbs of a gluten-free combination of all-purpose and specialty flour (such as King Arthur)
4. 2 Cups milk
5. nutmeg, ground, one-fourth teaspoon
6. 2 Cups shredded cheddar cheese
7. To taste, salt and pepper is available.

Steps To Cook: To Cook:

1. First, cook the gluten-free elbow macaroni as directed per the package's Steps To Cook:.
2. In a large saucepan over medium heat, melt the butter without adding any salt.
3. Whisk in the gluten-free all-purpose flour mix until a smooth consistency is achieved.
4. Gradually add the nutmeg while whisking in the milk.
5. Bring the mixture to a simmer and thicken over low heat, whisking constantly.
6. When the cheese is melted and smooth, remove the pan from the heat and toss in the shredded cheddar cheese.
7. 7 You may season it with salt and pepper to taste.
8. Eight, after the pasta is done cooking, drain it and add it to the cheese sauce.
9. Nine, toss so as to coat.

23. Chicken Caesar Salad

Ingredients

1. 2 chicken breasts that have been removed of the bones and skin.
2. 2 Tbs. olive oil
3. 1 milligram of garlic powder
4. To taste, salt and pepper is available.
5. 8 Cups chopped romaine lettuce
6. 1/2 Cups of croutons that are gluten-free
7. Grated parmesan cheese equaling one-half Cups
8. 1/2 Cups Caesar dressing (make sure it is gluten-free)

Steps To Cook:

1. First, preheat the oven to 375 degrees F.
2. Second, line a baking sheet with parchment paper.
3. The chicken breasts should be coated in olive oil, then seasoned with garlic powder, salt, and pepper.
4. Cook the chicken for 25 to 30 minutes in a preheated oven, or until an instant-read thermometer registers 165 degrees Fahrenheit, whichever comes first.
5. Allow the chicken to rest for five minutes before slicing.
6. In a large bowl, combine the romaine lettuce, gluten-free croutons, and grated Parmesan cheese.
7. 7 Toss with Caesar salad dressing and serve.
8. Divide the salad among four dishes for serving.
9. Cover the tops of the plates with the sliced chicken.
10. When finished cooking, serve immediately.

24. Gluten-Free Meatballs

Ingredients Needed:

1. 1 pound ground beef
2. 1/2 Cups gluten-free breadcrumbs
3. 1 egg and a quarter Cups of grated Parmesan cheese
4. 1/4 Cups of fresh parsley that has been chopped
5. 1 milligram of garlic powder
6. To taste, salt and pepper is available.
7. 2 Cups gluten-free marinara sauce

Steps To Cook: To Cook:

1. First, preheat the oven to 375 degrees F.
2. Second, line a baking sheet with parchment paper.
3. Thirdly, in a sizable bowl, combine the ground beef, gluten-free breadcrumbs, grated Parmesan cheese, egg, fresh chopped parsley, garlic powder, salt, and pepper.
4. Keep stirring until everything is evenly combined.
5. Roll each meatball into a ball about the size of a golf ball, and then go to Step 5.
6. Spread the meatballs out in a single layer on the prepared baking sheet.
7. Then, after preheating the oven, put the meal in for 20 to 25 minutes.
8. In a large saucepan over medium heat, reheat gluten-free marinara sauce.
9. Add the meatballs to the sauce after they have cooked for an additional 10 to 15 minutes.
10. Serve immediately over zucchini noodles or gluten-free spaghetti.

25. Gluten-Free Pizza

Ingredients

1. 1 package of gluten-free pizza crust mix
2. 1/2 Cups tomato sauce
3. 1 Cups shredded mozzarella cheese
4. 1/2 Cups sliced pepperoni
5. a quarter of a Cups of sliced black olives
6. a quarter of a Cups of sliced red onion
7. 1 Tbs olive oil
8. To taste, salt and pepper is available

Steps To Cook:

1. Step one: preheat the oven to 425 degrees F.
2. Follow the package directions for making the gluten-free pizza dough.
3. Third, put the dough to a pizza pan after rolling it out on a floured surface.
4. Fourth, cover the crust with tomato sauce, but stop one inch from the edge.
5. The fifth step is to top the tomato sauce with the shredded mozzarella cheese.
6. Before serving, top the pizza with pepperoni slices, black olives, and red onion.
7. After seasoning the toppings with salt and pepper, sprinkle olive oil over them.
8. The golden crust may be achieved by baking the pizza for 15 to 20 minutes in a preheated oven.

26. Gluten-Free Pasta

Ingredients Needed:

1. 1 packet gluten-free pasta (such as Barilla)
2. 2 Tbs. olive oil
3. 1 garlic clove, finely chopped
4. 1/4 tsp. red pepper flakes
5. 1 can diced tomatoes
6. To taste, salt and pepper is available.
7. 1/4 Cups of fresh basil that has been chopped

Steps To Cook: To Cook:

1. Follow the package directions for cooking the gluten-free pasta.
2. Second, heat the olive oil in a large pan over medium heat.
3. Third, keep cooking the mixture for one more minute after adding the minced garlic and red pepper flakes.
4. Reduce the heat to a simmer after you've added the diced tomatoes.
5. Season with salt and pepper to taste. 5.
6. Six, maintain a low simmer for 10 to 15 minutes, or until the sauce reaches the desired consistency.
7. Mix the cooked pasta with the tomato sauce and the chopped basil.
8. Serve hot or warm immediately after cooking.

27. Gluten-Free Bread

Ingredients Needed:

1. 2 Cups of gluten-free flour mix suitable for all purposes (such as King Arthur)
2. 1/2 Cups almond flour
3. 2 teaspoons of dry instant yeast
4. 1 tsp salt 1 tsp sugar
5. 2 eggs
6. 1/4 Cups olive oil
7. 1 standard Cups of hot water

Steps To Cook: To Cook:

1. First, in a large bowl, whisk together the gluten-free all-purpose flour mix, almond flour, quick yeast, salt, and sugar.
2. In a second bowl, whisk together the eggs, olive oil, and boiling water.
3. Pour the liquid ingredients into the dry and stir until a sticky dough forms.
4. The dough has to rise for an hour in a warm, draft-free place after step 4, after the bowl has been covered with plastic wrap.
5. Preheat oven to 375 degrees F.
6. Parchment paper should be laid out on a baking pan.
7. Shape the dough into a round loaf and transfer it to the prepared baking sheet using a spatula.
8. Put the bread in a preheated oven for 35-40 minutes, or until the crust is a deep golden colour.
9. Remove the bread from the oven and let it rest for ten minutes before slicing and serving.

28. Quinoa Salad

Ingredients Needed:

1. 1 Cups quinoa
2. 2 ounces of water
3. 1/2 Cups diced cucumber
4. 1/2 Cups chopped tomato
5. 1/4 Cups of red onion that has been diced.
6. 1/4 Cups of fresh parsley that has been chopped
7. 2 Tbs olive oil
8. 2 Tbs lemon juice
9. To taste, salt and pepper

Steps To Cook: To Cook:

1. After giving the quinoa a quick rinse in a sieve with a fine mesh, place it in a medium-sized pot.
2. After adding the water, bring the mixture to a boil.
3. Once the water has been absorbed and the quinoa has reached the desired consistency, turn the heat down to low, cover the pan, and let it simmer for 15–20 minutes.
4. Take the pan off the heat, and then wait ten minutes before touching it again.
5. Mix together the quinoa that has been cooked, cucumber, tomato, red onion, and parsley in a large bowl.
6. Olive oil and fresh lemon juice should be mixed together in a separate basin using a whisk.
7. After pouring the dressing over the quinoa salad, toss it to evenly cover the quinoa.
8. Salt and pepper may be added to taste as a seasoning.
9. You may serve the dish either cold or at room temperature.

29. Lentil Soup

Ingredients Needed:

1. 1 Cups green lentils
2. 4 Cups of broth made from vegetables
3. 1 onion, cut into small pieces; 2 carrots, peeled and cut into small pieces; 2 stalks of celery, cut into small pieces; 2 cloves of garlic, minced; 1 tsp.of dried thyme
4. To taste, salt and pepper

Steps To Cook: To Cook:

1. After giving them a quick rinse in a sieve with a fine mesh, place the lentils in a big pot.
2. Mix in the thyme, garlic, onion, carrots, and celery along with the vegetable broth.
3. Over high heat, the mixture should be brought to a boil.
4. Once the lentils have reached the desired consistency, remove the pan from the heat, cover it, and let it simmer for 20–25 minutes.
5. Salt and pepper may be added to taste as a seasoning.
6. Serve piping hot with toast that is free of gluten.

30.　Stir-fry with Chicken

Ingredients Needed:

1. 1 pound of chicken breasts, boneless and skinless, cut; 2 Tbs of vegetable oil
2. 2 garlic cloves, chopped or minced
3. 1 tsp grated ginger
4. 1 sliced red bell pepper, 1 sliced yellow bell pepper, 1 Cups of sliced mushrooms
5. 1/4 Cups of soy sauce that is gluten-free
6. 2 teaspoons of honey
7. 1 level tsp.of cornstarch
8. To taste, salt and pepper is available.

Steps To Cook: To Cook:

1. The vegetable oil should be heated to a high temperature in a big pan.
2. Add the sliced chicken and continue to cook for another three to four minutes, or until the chicken is browned.
3. Sauté the garlic and ginger for one minute after adding them to the pan.
4. Sauté the sliced bell peppers and mushrooms for three to four minutes, or until they reach the desired tenderness.
5. Combine the honey, cornstarch, and gluten-free soy sauce in a small bowl and stir together until smooth.
6. After pouring the sauce into the pan, give it a good toss to cover everything.
7. Salt and pepper may be added to taste as a seasoning.
8. Serve immediately over hot rice or quinoa.

31. Baked Salmon

Ingredients Needed:

1. 4 salmon fillets
2. 2 Tbs. olive oil
3. 2 garlic cloves, chopped or minced
4. 1 tsp. dried thyme
5. To taste, salt and pepper is available.

Steps To Cook: To Cook:

1. Turn the oven up to 400 degrees Fahrenheit.
2. A baking sheet should be prepared with parchment paper.
3. Arrange the salmon fillets in a single layer on the baking sheet that has been prepared.
4. Olive oil, garlic, and thyme should be mixed together in a small basin using a whisk.
5. Sprinkle the combined ingredients all over the.
6. Use a brush to distribute it over so that it is uniformly coated.
7. To your desired taste, season the salmon with salt and pepper.
8. Bake the salmon in an oven that has been warmed for 12 to 15 minutes, or until it is fully cooked through and flakes readily when tested with a fork.
9. Serve while still hot, accompanied with roasted veggies on the side.

32.   Vegetable Curry

Ingredients Needed:

1. 1 Tbs vegetable oil
2. 1 onion, diced
3. 2 garlic cloves, chopped or minced
4. 1 tsp grated ginger
5. 2 carrots, peeled and cut into small pieces.
6. 2 potatoes, peeled and chopped into small pieces
7. 1 seeded and sliced red bell pepper
8. 1 can diced tomatoes
9. 1 chickpea can, drained and washed before serving
10. 1 Cups of vegetable broth
11. 1 tsp.of curry powder Ingredients Needed:
12. To taste, salt and pepper

Steps To Cook: To Cook:

1. Warm the vegetable oil in a large saucepan by heating it over a medium flame.
2. Sauté the onion, garlic, and ginger for two to three minutes, or until the onion and garlic have softened.
3. After adding the carrots, potatoes, and bell pepper, continue to sauté the mixture for another 5-7 minutes, or until the vegetables are soft.
4. The curry powder, chickpeas, diced tomatoes, and vegetable broth should all be added now.
5. Salt and pepper may be added to taste as a seasoning.
6. Over high heat, the mixture should be brought to a boil.
7. Cover the pot, bring the mixture to a simmer over low heat, and cook for 20–25 minutes, or until the veggies are tender all the way through.
8. Serve hot with naan or rice that does not contain gluten.

33. Gluten-Free Pancakes

Ingredients Needed:

1. 1 Cups of a gluten-free all-purpose flour mix that is not containing gluten
2. 1 Tbs sugar
3. 2 tsp baking powder
4. 1/2 tsp salt
5. 1 egg
6. 1 Cups milk
7. 2 Tbs vegetable oil

Steps To Cook: To Cook:

1. First, whisk together a big bowl's worth of gluten-free all-purpose flour blend, sugar, baking powder, and salt.
2. In another dish, thoroughly blend the egg, milk, and vegetable oil using a whisk.
3. Add the liquid ingredients to the dry and continue whisking until the mixture is entirely smooth.
4. In a pan that won't stick, preheat it over medium heat.
5. Using a quarter Cups for each pancake, pour the batter onto the griddle. 5. Cook the pancakes for about three minutes on each side, or until they reach a golden brown color, on a griddle or frying pan.
6. Seven, accompany the hot meal with butter and maple syrup as soon as possible."

"Soup

34. Tomato Soup

Ingredients

1. 2 Tbs olive oil
2. 1 onion, diced
3. 2 garlic cloves, chopped or minced
4. 2 cans (28 oz each) chopped tomatoes
5. 2 measuring Cups of chicken broth and 1 measuring Cups of heavy cream
6. To taste, salt and pepper is available.

Steps To Cook: To Cook:

1. Warm the olive oil in a large saucepan by heating it over a medium flame.
2. After adding the onion and garlic, sauté them for about two to three minutes, or until the onion has softened.
3. To the pot, add the chicken stock and diced tomatoes.
4. Bring the mixture all the way up to a boil, and then turn the heat down to a low setting.
5. Simmer the soup for 20 to 25 minutes, or until it has reached the desired consistency.

6. Take the saucepan from the heat and, using an immersion blender, purée the soup until it reaches a smooth consistency.
7. Mix in the heavy cream, and then season to taste with salt and freshly ground pepper.
8. To be served hot.

35. Chicken Noodle Soup

Ingredients Needed:

1. 1 pound of chicken breasts that are boneless and skinless
2. 1 Tbs olive oil
3. 1 onion, diced
4. 2 garlic cloves, chopped or minced
5. 6 Cups of chicken broth 2 Cups of egg noodles that are gluten-free
6. 2 Cups of carrots, thinly sliced
7. 2 Cups of celery, thinly sliced
8. 1 tsp dried thyme
9. To taste, salt and pepper is available.

Steps To Cook: To Cook:

1. Prepare the oven to 375 degrees Fahrenheit.
2. Olive oil should be used to coat the chicken breasts, and then salt and pepper should be added to taste.
3. Bake the chicken in an oven that has been warmed for 25 to 30 minutes, or until it reaches an internal temperature of 165 degrees Fahrenheit.
4. Before slicing the chicken, let it a rest for five minutes first.
5. In a large saucepan, heat the olive oil over medium heat and sauté the minced garlic and chopped onion for about two to three minutes, or until the onion has softened.
6. In a saucepan, combine the chicken broth, gluten-free egg noodles, sliced carrots, sliced celery, and dried thyme.
7. Keep the soup at a simmer for about ten to fifteen minutes, or until the veggies are fork-tender and the noodles are fully cooked.
8. Simmer the soup for a further 5 minutes after adding the sliced chicken and then remove the soup from the heat.
9. Salt and pepper may be added to taste as a seasoning.
10. To be served hot.

36. French onion soup

Ingredients

1. 4 Tbs unsalted butter
2. 4 onions, cut as thinly as possible
3. 1 Tbs of a gluten-free combination of all-purpose and specialty flour (such as King Arthur)
4. 4 measuring Cups of beef broth
5. 1 Tbs balsamic vinegar
6. To taste, salt and pepper is available.
7. 4 slices of bread that is gluten-free
8. Half of shredded Gruyère cheese

Steps To Cook:

1. In a big pot that is set over medium heat, butter should be melted without any more salt being added.
2. After adding the thinly sliced onions, continue to sauté the onions for another 20 to 25 minutes, or until they have turned a golden brown colour and caramelised.
3. The gluten-free all-purpose flour mix ought to be dusted over the onions, and then the mixture ought to be mixed so that everything can be combined.
4. Add the beef broth and the balsamic vinegar in a slow and steady stream while stirring constantly.
5. Maintain a low simmer in the soup for around ten to fifteen minutes, or until it has reached the desired thickness.
6. As a form of seasoning, salt and pepper can be sprinkled on the food as desired.
7. Get the grill ready in the oven.
8. Toast the pieces of gluten-free bread in the toaster or under the grill until they are just slightly golden.
9. Place the soup in oven-safe bowls so it can be heated in the oven.
10. A piece of gluten-free bread that has been toasted on top of each cup of soup is something that ought to be included.
11. It is recommended that shredded Gruyère cheese be spread across the top of the loaf of bread.

12. Put the soup bowls under the grill for two to three minutes, or until the cheese has melted, depending on how quickly you want your soup.
13. Served in a blazing hot state.

37. Gluten-Free Minestrone Soup

Ingredients Needed:

1. 2 Tbs olive oil
2. 1 onion, diced
3. 2 garlic cloves, chopped or minced
4. 2 Cups chopped potatoes
5. 2 Cups chopped carrots
6. 2 Cups of celery cut into dice
7. 1 can (28 oz) chopped tomatoes
8. 6 gallons of vegetable stock
9. 1 can of cannellini beans, drained and washed, weighing 15 ounces total
10. 1 Cups gluten-free pasta (such as elbow or rotini)
11. 1 tsp dried basil
12. 1 tsp dried oregano
13. To taste, salt and pepper is available.

Steps To Cook: To Cook:

1. To preheat the olive oil, place it in a large saucepan and set it over a hob with a medium flame.
2. When you've added the onion and garlic, give the mixture a quick sauté for around two to three minutes, or until the onion has become more tender.
3. At this stage, you should cut the potatoes, carrots, and celery into cubes and add them to the dish.
4. Sauté the vegetables for about five to seven minutes, or until they are just beginning to get soft, depending on how long you want them to take.
5. Both the diced tomatoes and the vegetable broth should be placed inside of the saucepan.
6. After bringing the mixture all the way up to a boil, reduce the heat to a low setting and let it simmer for a few minutes.
7. Maintain a low simmer in the soup for fifteen to twenty minutes, or until the vegetables have acquired the desired degree of softness.

8. Cannellini beans that have been drained and rinsed before being added to the soup along with gluten-free pasta, dried basil, and dried oregano are the other ingredients that should be used.
9. Maintaining a low simmer in the broth for an additional ten to fifteen minutes, or until the pasta has attained the doneness you choose, is the next step.
10. As a form of seasoning, salt and pepper can be sprinkled on the food as desired.
11. To be consumed while heated.

38. Gluten-Free Greek Salad

Ingredients Needed:

1. 6 Cups chopped romaine lettuce
2. 2 Cups of cucumber that has been chopped.
3. 2 Cups of tomato chunks, diced
4. 1/2 of a red onion, cut very thinly
5. 1/2 Cups pitted Kalamata olives
6. 1/2 Cups of feta cheese in crushed form
7. 1/4 Cups of fresh parsley that has been chopped
8. 2 Tbs fresh lemon juice
9. 2 teaspoons of vinegar made from red wine
10. 1/4 Cups olive oil
11. 1 tsp dried oregano
12. To taste, salt and pepper is available.

Steps To Cook: To Cook:

1. Place the chopped romaine lettuce in a large bowl and blend it with the other ingredients, includes diced cucumber, chopped tomato, thinly sliced red onion, pitted Kalamata olives, crumbled feta cheese, and chopped fresh parsley.
2. To create the dressing, place the fresh lemon juice, red wine vinegar, olive oil, dried oregano, and a pinch each of salt and pepper in a separate dish and whisk all of the ingredients together.
3. Combine the salad with the dressing by tossing.
4. Immediately serve after cooking.

39.　Gluten-Free Broccoli Salad

Ingredients Needed:

1. 4 Cups of broccoli florets that have been chopped
2. 1/2 Cups raisins
3. 1/2 Tbs of chopped bacon 1 Tbs of chopped red onion
4. 1/2 Cups mayonnaise
5. 14 of a Cups of honey
6. 2 Tbs apple cider vinegar
7. To taste, salt and pepper is available.

Steps To Cook: To Cook:

1. Mix the broccoli florets, raisins, bacon, and red onion that have been diced together in a large bowl.
2. To prepare the dressing, put the mayonnaise, honey, apple cider vinegar, salt, and pepper into a separate dish and mix all of the ingredients together.
3. Combine the salad with the dressing by tossing.
4. Before serving, place the salad in the refrigerator for at least half an hour to let it chill.

40. Gluten-Free Taco Salad

Ingredients Needed:

1. 1 pound ground beef
2. 1 onion, diced
3. 2 cloves of garlic, minced 1 can of black beans (15 ounces), drained and washed 1 can of corn (15 ounces), drained and rinsed
4. 1/2 Cups of fresh cilantro that has been chopped.
5. 1/4 Cups fresh lime juice
6. To taste, salt and pepper is available.
7. 6 Cups chopped romaine lettuce
8. 1 Cups of tomato chunks, chopped
9. 1 Cups shredded cheddar cheese
10. 1 Cups of tortilla chips that are gluten-free

Steps To Cook: To Cook:

1. Cook the ground beef in a large pan over medium heat until it has a browned appearance.
2. After adding the onion and garlic, sauté them for about two to three minutes, or until the onion has softened.
3. Add the black beans, which have been drained and washed, along with the corn, which has also been drained, to the pan.
4. Mix in the finely chopped fresh cilantro, as well as the freshly squeezed lime juice.
5. Salt and pepper may be added to taste as a seasoning.
6. Mix the gluten-free tortilla chips, shredded cheddar cheese, chopped romaine lettuce, and diced tomato in a large dish. Mix in the chopped romaine lettuce.
7. Place the ground beef and bean mixture on top of the salad.
8. Immediately serve after cooking.

41. Gluten-Free Caprese Salad

Ingredients Needed:

1. 1/3 Cups of finely chopped fresh basil leaves 4 big tomatoes, cut 1 pound of fresh mozzarella cheese, sliced
2. 2 Tbs balsamic vinegar
3. 2 Tbs olive oil
4. To taste, salt and pepper is available.

Steps To Cook: To Cook:

1. Prepare a dish for serving and arrange the tomato slices and fresh mozzarella cheese slices on it.
2. The fresh basil leaves, chopped, should be sprinkled on top of the tomatoes and cheese.
3. To prepare the dressing, put the balsamic vinegar, olive oil, salt, and pepper into a small bowl and mix all of the ingredients together.
4. The salad should be drizzled with the dressing before serving.
5. Immediately serve after cooking.

42. Gluten-Free Waldorf salad

Ingredients Needed:

1. 4 Cups chopped romaine lettuce
2. 2 Cups of apple pieces, chopped
3. 1 fluid ounce of chopped celery
4. 1/2 Cups of walnuts that have been chopped
5. 1/2 Cups raisins
6. 1/2 Cups mayonnaise
7. 1 Tbs fresh lemon juice
8. 1 Tbs of honey
9. To taste, salt and pepper is available.

Steps To Cook: To Cook:

1. Put the chopped romaine lettuce, chopped apples, chopped celery, chopped walnuts, and raisins in a big bowl and mix it all together.
2. In a separate bowl, combine the mayonnaise, fresh lemon juice, and salt and pepper to taste.
3. To prepare the dressing, you will need the juice, honey, salt, and pepper.
4. Add the dressing to the salad and toss to combine.
5. Before serving, place the salad in the refrigerator for at least half an hour to let it chill."

"Meat and sea foods

43. Garlic and lemon rubbed shrimp skewers

Ingredients Needed:

1. 1 pound of shrimp, cleaned (peeled and deveined), and left uncooked 14 Cups olive oil
2. 3 garlic cloves, chopped into small pieces
3. 2 Tbs of juice extracted from fresh lemons
4. a quarter of a tsp. of salt
5. pepper, black, one-fourth of a teaspoon
6. Wooden skewers (soaked in water for at least 30 minutes)

Steps To Cook::

1. Prepare the grill for cooking over medium-high heat.
2. Olive oil, garlic, lemon juice, salt, and black pepper should be mixed together in a small bowl using a whisk.
3. Skewer the shrimp, being sure to distribute them equally between the skewers.
4. Coat the shrimp skewers with the olive oil and garlic mixture and set aside.

5. Put the skewers on the grill and cook them for about two to three minutes on each side, or until the shrimp are pink and completely cooked through.
6. Serve steaming hot with extra slices of lemon.

Nutritional Value

- Calories: 202
- Fat: 14g
- Protein: 18g
- Carbohydrates: 1g
- Fiber: 0g
- Sugar: 0g

44.   Mustard and rosemary rubbed chicken thighs

Ingredients Needed:

1. 4 chicken thighs with the bones in and the skin on
2. 2 teaspoons of mustard made with Dijon
3. 1 table spoon of mustard made with whole grains
4. 1 tsp.of extra-virgin olive oil
5. 2 garlic cloves, chopped, and set aside.
6. 1 Tbs of freshly chopped rosemary
7. To taste, salt and black pepper will be used.

Steps To Cook::

1. Turn the oven up to 400 degrees Fahrenheit.
2. Mix the two types of mustard, the olive oil, the garlic, and the rosemary in a small bowl using a whisk.
3. Put the chicken thighs on an oven-safe dish, and then brush the mustard mixture all over the chicken, being sure to equally cover each thigh.
4. The chicken should be seasoned with both salt and black pepper.
5. Cook the chicken in the oven for 30 to 35 minutes, or until it is completely cooked through and browned.
6. Serve hot with the gluten-free food of your choice that does not contain gluten.

NutritionalValue

- Calories: 356
- Fat: 25g
- Protein: 30g
- Carbohydrates: 2g
- Fiber: 0g
- Sugar: 0g

45. Salmon skewers grilled with avocado salsa.

Ingredients Needed:

1. 4 salmon fillets
2. 2 teaspoons of extra-virgin olive oil
3. To taste, salt and black pepper will be used.
4. 2 perfectly ripe avocados, one-half of a red onion sliced, one-fourth of a Cups of fresh cilantro, chopped, and one lime, juiced
5. To taste, salt and black pepper will be used.

Steps To Cook:

1. To begin, get a grill going over a heat setting somewhere in the middle.
2. First, the salmon fillets should be seasoned with salt and black pepper, and then they should be covered in olive oil.
3. In the third step, place the salmon on the grill and cook it for about five minutes each side, or until it flakes easily and is completely done.
4. While the salmon is being grilled, prepare the avocado topping by combining chopped avocados, red onion, cilantro, lime juice, salt and black pepper on a platter.
5. Accompany the salmon fillets that have been grilled with an abundant helping of avocado salsa.

Nutritional Value

- Calories: 425
- Fat: 29g
- Protein: 32g
- Carbohydrates: 14g
- Fiber: 9g
- Sugar: 2g"

Desserts

46. Chocolate Chip Cookies

Ingredients Needed:

1. 1 Cups unsalted butter, at room temperature
2. 1 Cups granulated sugar
3. 2 large eggs
4. 2 teaspoons vanilla extract
5. 2 Cups of gluten-free all-purpose flour mix
6. 1 tsp.baking soda
7. 1 tsp.salt
8. 2 Cups semisweet chocolate chips

Steps To Cook: To Cook:

1. The first step is to preheat the oven to 190 degrees Celsius (375 F).
2. Place the sugar and butter in a large bowl and use an electric mixer to whisk the ingredients together until the mixture is fluffy and light.
3. After beating in each egg one at a time, include the vanilla extract by whisking it in after the eggs have been incorporated.

4. Put the flour, baking soda and salt into a separate bowl and whisk them together until they are completely incorporated.
5. Gradually add the dry ingredients to the butter mixture while continuing to thoroughly combine the ingredients after each addition.
6. Mix the chocolate chips with the peanut butter in a separate bowl.
7. Form the dough into balls with a diameter of about one inch and arrange them in a single layer on a baking sheet that has been previously prepared.
8. Continue baking for an additional ten to twelve minutes, or until the edges are starting to acquire a golden brown colour.
9. Before serving, let to cool on a wire rack for a few minutes.

Nutritional Info:

- Calories: 207
- Fat: 11g
- Carbohydrates: 26g
- Protein: 2g

47. Strawberry Shortcake

Ingredients Needed:

1. 1 quart fresh strawberries, hulled and sliced
2. 1/4 Cups granulated sugar
3. 2 Cups of gluten-free all-purpose flour mix
4. 1/4 Cups granulated sugar
5. 1 Tbs baking powder
6. 1/2 tsp.salt
7. 1/2 Cups unsalted butter, chilled and cubed
8. 1/2 Cups milk
9. Whipped cream, for serving

Steps To Cook: To Cook:

1. First, heat the oven to 425 degrees Fahrenheit (218 degrees C).
2. Second, place the strawberries in a medium basin and whisk in the remaining 1/4 Cups of sugar.
3. In a large bowl, whisk together the flour, 1/4 Cups sugar, baking powder, and salt.
4. Step 4: Cut the butter into the flour mixture using a pastry blender until the mixture resembles coarse crumbs.
5. After the dough has formed, add more milk a little at a time while stirring.
6. Transfer the dough to a floured work area and knead briefly.
7. Roll out the dough to a thickness of half an inch, and then use a biscuit cutter to cut out circles.
8. Place the rounds, one by one, on a baking sheet lined with parchment paper, and bake for 12 to 15 minutes, or until golden brown.
9. Bring the shortcakes to room temperature before serving with the strawberries and whipped topping.

Nutritional Info:

- Calories: 329
- Fat: 16g
- Carbohydrates: 44g
- Protein: 4g

48. Chocolate Brownies

Ingredients Needed:

1. 1 Cups unsalted butter
2. 2 Cups granulated sugar
3. 4 large eggs
4. 2 teaspoons vanilla extract
5. 2/3 Cups unsweetened cocoa powder
6. 1 Cups of gluten-free all-purpose flour mix
7. 1/2 tsp.salt
8. 1/2 tsp.baking powder

Steps To Cook: To Cook:

1. Place in the oven and immediately increase the temperature to 175 degrees Celsius (or 350 degrees Fahrenheit).
2. Two, start by melting the butter in a pot of medium size over low heat.
3. Add the sugar and continue whisking until there are no lumps in the batter.
4. Take the pan from the burner, add the eggs and the vanilla essence, and whisk constantly until everything is incorporated.
5. Fifth, fold the cocoa powder, flour, salt, and baking powder into the wet ingredients until they are evenly distributed.
6. Transfer the batter to a baking dish that is buttered and measures 9 by 13 inches.
7. After 25 to 30 minutes in the oven, you should be able to remove a toothpick that was placed in the middle without any residue. 7. Allow the meat to cool for an adequate amount of time before slicing and serving it.

Nutritional Info:

- Calories: 352
- Fat: 18g
- Carbohydrates: 47g
- Protein: 4g

49. Banana Bread

Ingredients Needed:

1. Three mashed ripe bananas
2. a half Cups of melted unsalted butter
3. ounces of white sugar
4. To wit: 4 big eggs
5. One vanilla extract teaspoon
6. 1-and-a-half Cups of gluten-free all-purpose flour mix
7. baking soda, teaspoon
8. milligrammes of salt

Steps To Cook: To Cook:

1. Set the oven temperature to 175 degrees Celsius (350 degrees Fahrenheit).
2. In a large bowl, combine the mashed bananas, sugar, eggs, melted butter, and vanilla essence.
3. Mix the flour, baking soda and salt together until they are completely incorporated.
4. Transfer the batter to a loaf pan measuring 9 by 5 inches that has been oiled.
5. Bake for 50 to 60 minutes, or until a toothpick inserted in the centre comes out clean. If using a timer, start checking at the 50 minute mark.
6. Ten minutes of cooling time should be spent in the pan, after which the brownies should be moved to a wire rack to finish cooling.

Nutritional Info:

- Calories: 279
- Fat: 12g
- Carbohydrates: 40g
- Protein: 4g

50.   Lemon Bars

Ingredients Needed:

1. 1 Cups of unsalted butter, softened at room temperature
2. 2 Cups of all-purpose flour
3. 1/2 Cups of powdered sugar
4. 1/4 tsp.of salt
5. 4 big eggs
6. 1 1/2 Cups of granulated sugar
7. 1/4 Cups of gluten-free all-purpose flour mix
8. 2/3 Cups of freshly squeezed lemon juice
9. Powdered sugar for dusting

Steps To Cook: To Cook:

1. Preset oven temperature to 175 degrees C (350 degrees F).
2. In a large bowl, beat together the butter, flour, powdered sugar, and salt until the mixture resembles crumbly bread crumbs.
3. Press the mixture down firmly into a baking dish that is 9 inches by 13 inches and has been greased.
4. Cook for twenty minutes, or until a golden colour has developed, whichever comes first.
5. While the crust bakes, combine the eggs, granulated sugar, flour, and lemon juice in a mixing bowl and whisk until smooth.
6. Take the crust out of the oven and spread it with the lemon mixture after it has cooled.
7. Continue baking for another 25 to 30 minutes, or until it reaches the desired consistency.
8. Once the brownies have cooled completely, dust them with powdered sugar and cut them into squares.

Nutritional Info:

- Calories: 311
- Fat: 15g
- Carbohydrates: 43g
- Protein: 3g

51. Oatmeal Raisin Cookies

Ingredients Needed:

1. 1 Cups of room-temperature unsalted butter
2. 2 Tbs of brown sugar
   - Two big eggs
3. 4 - Vanilla extract, 2 teaspoons
4. One and a half Cups of gluten-free all-purpose flour mix
5. 6 - A baking soda, 1 tsp.
6. A half tsp.of salt
7. 8 servings (3 Cups) of traditional rolled oats
8. Amount: 1 Cups raisins

Steps To Cook: To Cook:

1. Preheat the oven to 175 degrees Celsius (350 Fahrenheit).
2. In a large basin, use a hand mixer to cream together the butter and brown sugar until the mixture is light and fluffy.
3. While continuing to beat, add the eggs one at a time, and then whisk in the vanilla extract.
4. A second bowl should be used to combine the dry ingredients of baking powder, salt, and flour.
5. Combine the wet and dry ingredients well after adding them to the butter.
6. You should thoroughly combine the rolled oats and the raisins in a single bowl.
7. Scoop the dough onto a baking sheet that has been prepared with parchment paper using rounded tablespoons and space them roughly 2 inches apart.
8. Bake at 350° for 12–15 minutes, or until brown.
9. After allowing the food to cool on a wire rack, serve.

Nutritional Info:

- Calories: 259
- Fat: 12g
- Carbohydrates: 36g
- Protein: 4g

Cakes

52. Classic Vanilla Cake

Ingredients Needed:

1. 2 Cups of gluten-free all-purpose flour mix
2. 2 teaspoons baking powder
3. 1/2 tsp.salt
4. 1 1/2 Cups granulated sugar
5. 3/4 Cups whole milk
6. 2 large eggs
7. 2 teaspoons vanilla extract
8. 1/2 Cups unsalted butter, at room temperature

Steps To Cook: To Cook:

1. Adjust the thermostat in the oven so that it reads 175 degrees Celsius (350 degrees Fahrenheit).
2. Spread some butter and flour in each of the two cake pans, and make sure they are at least 9 inches in diameter.

3. Before continuing with the recipe, the dry ingredients, including flour, sugar, baking soda and salt, should all be combined in a large basin using a stirring motion.
4. After adding the milk, eggs, butter, and vanilla essence, continue to mix the ingredients until they are completely incorporated into one another.
5. It is essential to make sure that the cake batter is spread out evenly throughout all of the pans.
6. If the toothpick reveals raw food on it, cooking should be continued for another five minutes.
7. After ten minutes, remove the cakes from the pans and set them on a wire rack so that they may finish cooling off.
8. Make sure the icing and the decorations are exactly how you want them.

Nutritional Info:

- Calories: 303
- Fat: 10g
- Carbohydrates: 50g
- Protein: 4g

53. Chocolate Cake

Ingredients Needed:

1. 2 Cups of gluten-free all-purpose flour mix
2. 3/4 Cups unsweetened cocoa powder
3. 2 large eggs
4. 2 Cups granulated sugar
5. 2 teaspoons baking soda
6. 1 tsp. baking powder
7. 1 tsp.salt
8. 1 Cups buttermilk
9. 1/2 Cups vegetable oil
10. 2 teaspoons vanilla extract
11. 1 Cups hot water

Steps To Cook: To Cook:

1. The first step is to preheat the oven to 175 C (350 F).
2. If you want to make two 9-inch cakes, you'll need to oil and flour two pans.
3. The dry ingredients (flour, sugar, cocoa powder, baking soda, baking powder and salt) should be whisked together in a large bowl. All of the ingredients need to go into the basin.
4. Whisk the buttermilk, eggs, vanilla extract, and vegetable oil together in a large basin until the batter is smooth and uniform in texture.
5. Slowly add the hot water into the basin while kneading the dough continually. Do this until the batter is totally smooth, which may take some time.
6. After step 5, when the cake pans are ready, pour the mixture into them and spread it out evenly with a spatula.
7. A toothpick inserted in the middle should come out clean after about 35 minutes of baking.
8. If you're using a timer, wait 30 minutes before starting the inspections.
9. Wait 10 minutes after taking the cakes out of the oven to make sure they have cooled completely in the pans before placing them to a wire rack to cool completely.

10. If you want to design the cake whatever you desire, you need frost it first.

Nutritional Info:

- Calories: 351
- Fat: 15g
- Carbohydrates: 53g
- Protein: 5g

54. Carrot Cake

Ingredients Needed:

1. 2 Cups of gluten-free all-purpose flour mix
2. 1 tsp. ground cinnamon
3. 1/2 tsp. ground nutmeg
4. 1/2 tsp. salt
5. 2 teaspoons baking powder
6. 1 1/2 teaspoons baking soda
7. 1 1/2 Cups granulated sugar
8. 1 Cups vegetable oil
9. 4 large eggs
10. 2 Cups grated carrots
11. 1 Cups chopped walnuts
12. Cream cheese frosting, for serving

Steps To Cook: To Cook:

1. Set the oven temperature to 175 degrees Celsius (350 degrees Fahrenheit).
2. Prepare two cake pans with a diameter of 9 inches by greasing and flouring them.
3. A big bowl should be used, and a whisk should be used to combine the following ingredients: flour, baking powder, baking soda, cinnamon and nutmeg.
4. when properly combining the sugar, eggs, and vegetable oil in a separate dish, leave this mixture away when it has been prepared.
5. Stirring together the grated carrots and chopped walnuts is the best way to combine the two ingredients.
6. Combine the dry ingredients with the wet ones in stages until you get the desired consistency.

Nutritional Info:

- Calories: 442
- Fat: 26g
- Carbohydrates: 48g
- Protein: 6g

55. Lemon Pound Cake

Ingredients Needed:

1. 1 1/2 Cups of gluten-free all-purpose flour mix
2. 1/2 tsp. baking powder
3. 1/2 tsp. baking soda
4. 1/2 tsp. salt
5. 1/2 Cups unsalted butter, at room temperature
6. 1 Cups granulated sugar
7. 2 large eggs
8. 1/2 Cups sour cream
9. 2 Tbs lemon zest
10. 2 Tbs freshly squeezed lemon juice

Steps To Cook:

1. The first step is to preheat the oven to 175 C (350 F).
2. Prepare a 9-by-5-inch loaf pan by greasing and flouring it and setting it aside.
3. Mix the dry ingredients (baking powder, baking soda and salt) in a large bowl using a whisk.
4. Put the butter and sugar in a separate basin and beat them together until they become light and airy.
5. After adding the eggs one at a time and mixing well after each addition, add the sour cream to the batter and then the lemon juice and zest.
6. Add the dry ingredients one at a time and stir regularly until they are all incorporated in step 6.
7. The batter is put into the prepared loaf pan.
8. Until a toothpick inserted in the middle comes out clean, bake for 45 to 50 minutes. Inspect the cake about ten minutes before it's done baking. Wait 30 minutes if you're using a timer, and then start checking.
9. After ten minutes of cooling in the prepared pan, remove the cake from the pan and place it on a wire rack to finish cooling.
10. You may serve the cake with either whipped cream or powdered sugar on top. Cut the cake into individual servings before serving.

Nutritional Info:

- Calories: 344
- Fat: 16g
- Carbohydrates: 47g
- Protein: 4g

56. Red Velvet Cake

Ingredients Needed:

1. 2 1/2 Cups of gluten-free cake flour
2. 1 1/2 Cups granulated sugar
3. 1 tsp.baking powder
4. 1 tsp.baking soda
5. 1 tsp.salt
6. 1 1/2 Cups vegetable oil
7. 1 Cups buttermilk
8. 2 large eggs
9. 2 tbs. red food coloring
10. 1 tsp. vanilla extract
11. 1 tsp. white vinegar
12. Cream cheese frosting, for serving

Steps To Cook:

1. First, keep cooking for another 5–7 minutes, until the pepper and mushrooms are soft
2. To get the appropriate tenderness, zucchini noodles should be cooked for two to three minutes.
3. To preheat the oven, dial in an internal temperature of 175 degrees Celsius (350 degrees Fahrenheit).
4. In two 9-inch cake pans, grease and flour the bottoms and sides.
5. In a large bowl, mix together the cake flour, sugar, baking powder, baking soda and salt.
6. Before adding to the batter, combine the other ingredients in a separate dish by whisking together the vegetable oil, buttermilk, eggs, red food coloring, vanilla essence, and white vinegar.
7. Seven, gradually add the dry ingredients while stirring frequently, and keep stirring until the mixture is smooth.
8. Pour the batter into the prepared cake pans in an even distribution.

9. A toothpick inserted in the middle should come out clean after 30–35 minutes in the oven.
10. Transfer the cakes to the wire rack and let them cool completely before serving. After ten minutes, remove the cakes from the pans and allow them to cool completely.
11. Use cream cheese frosting to cover the cakes, then decorate as you see suitable.

Nutritional Info:

- Calories: 552
- Fat: 35g
- Carbohydrates: 55g
- Protein: 6g

Vegetarian gluten-free recipe

57. Cauliflower Fried Rice

Ingredients Needed:

1. Salt and black pepper, to taste
2. 1 head cauliflower, grated or chopped into small pieces
3. 2 Tbs coconut oil
4. 2 garlic cloves, minced
5. 2 large eggs, beaten
6. 1/2 Cups diced carrots
7. 1/2 Cups frozen peas
8. 2 Tbs gluten-free soy sauce or tamari
9. 1/2 Cups diced onion
10. Green onions, sliced, for serving

Steps To Cook: To Cook:

1. Cook for another 5–7 minutes, or until the mushrooms and pepper are soft.
2. Noodles made from zucchini should be cooked for two to three minutes, or until soft.
3. To soften the mushrooms and pepper, continue cooking for another 5–7 minutes.

4. Zucchini noodles need just three minutes in the microwave to get tender.
5. Coconut oil should be melted over low to medium heat in a big pan.
6. Add the garlic and onion and sauté until the onion is translucent, around 2 to 3 minutes.
7. Add the vegetables and continue to sauté for another three to four minutes, or until the carrots and peas are tender.
8. For optimal softness, cauliflower should be cooked for around 7 minutes.
9. Remove the vegetables from the centre of the pan and set them around the outsides.
10. Scramble the eggs and then mix them in with the greens.
11. Mix in the tamari or gluten-free soy sauce, as well as salt and black pepper to taste.
12. Serve immediately with a sprinkling of chopped green onions.

Nutritional Info:

- Calories: 196
- Fat: 11g
- Carbohydrates: 18g
- Protein: 8g

58. Spinach and Feta Stuffed Sweet Potatoes

Ingredients Needed:

1. 2 Cups fresh spinach, chopped
2. 4 medium sweet potatoes
3. 2 garlic cloves, minced
4. 1/4 Cups crumbled feta cheese
5. 1 Tbs olive oil
6. 1 small onion, chopped
7. Salt and black pepper, to taste

Steps To Cook: To Cook:

1. Continue to cook for a further five to seven minutes, or until the pepper and mushrooms are tender.
2. Cooking zucchini noodles for two to three minutes, or until they reach the desired degree of softness, is recommended.
3. Continue cooking for another 5 to 7 minutes so that the pepper and mushrooms can become more pliable.
4. Cooking time for sweet potatoes should be between 45 and 50 minutes, or until the potatoes are soft, after being pierced with a fork.
5. Third, get the olive oil nice and toasty in a large saucepan by heating it over a low to medium heat.
6. In order to soften, zucchini noodles just need about two to three minutes in the microwave.
7. 5 Pre-heat the oven to 400 degrees Fahrenheit (200 degrees Celsius).
8. Step 6 calls for combining the mashed spinach and sweet potato together.
9. After adjusting the seasoning with black pepper and salt, add in some feta cheese.
10. Sauté the onion and garlic for about three minutes, or until the onion turns translucent, whichever comes first.
11. When the spinach has wilted, which should take around two to three minutes, add it to the boiling water.
12. 10 Make an incision down the middle of each sweet potato, and remove portion of the flesh with a spoon.

13. After refilling the sweet potatoes, immediately serve them with the spinach mixture that was previously inside.

Nutritional Info:

- Calories: 253
- Fat: 6g
- Carbohydrates: 45g
- Protein: 6g

59. Zucchini Noodle Stir-Fry

Ingredients Needed:

1. 2 Tbs cornstarch
2. 1/4 Cups chopped fresh cilantro
3. 4 medium zucchini, spiralized into noodles
4. 1 Tbs olive oil
5. 1 red bell pepper, sliced
6. 1/4 Cups gluten-free soy sauce or tamari
7. 1 small onion, chopped
8. 2 garlic cloves, minced
9. 2 Cups sliced mushrooms

Steps To Cook: To Cook:

1. Continue to cook for a further five to seven minutes, or until the pepper and mushrooms are tender.
2. Cooking zucchini noodles for two to three minutes, or until they reach the desired degree of softness, is recommended.
3. Continue cooking for another 5 to 7 minutes so that the pepper and mushrooms can become more pliable.
4. Cooking time for zucchini noodles should be between two and three minutes, or until the noodles are tender.
5. Third, in a small bowl, thoroughly combine the cornflour with the gluten-free soy sauce or tamari until you have a smooth consistency.
6. Warm the olive oil in a big saucepan on a heat setting between low and medium.
7. After adding the onion and garlic, continue to cook for another two to three minutes, or until the onion reaches a translucent state.
8. Toss the veggies to coat them in the soy sauce mixture after adding it to the pan with the vegetables.
9. Continue to cook for an additional minute or two so that the sauce can thicken.
10. Serve at once while it is still very hot, and sprinkle the top with some chopped cilantro.

Nutritional Info:

- Calories: 109
- Fat: 4g
- Carbohydrates: 15g
- Protein: 6g

CONVERSION MEASUREMENT TABLE

WEIGHT

IMPERIAL	METRIC
1/2 oz	15 g
1 oz	29 g
2 oz	57 g
3 oz	85 g
4 oz	113 g
5 oz	141 g
6 oz	170 g
8 oz	227 g
10 oz	283 g
12 oz	340 g
13 oz	369 g
14 oz	397 g
15 oz	425 g
1 lb	453 g

MEASUREMENT

CUP	ONCES	MILLILITERS	TABLESPOONS
8 cup	64 oz	1895 ml	128
6 cup	48 oz	1420 ml	96
5 cup	40 oz	1180 ml	80
4 cup	32 oz	960 ml	64
2 cup	16 oz	480 ml	32
1 cup	8 oz	240 ml	16
3/4 cup	6 oz	177 ml	12
2/3 cup	5 oz	158 ml	11
1/2 cup	4 oz	118 ml	8
3/8 cup	3 oz	90 ml	6
1/3 cup	2.5 oz	79 ml	5.5
1/4 cup	2 oz	59 ml	4
1/8 cup	1 oz	30 ml	3
1/16 cup	1/2 oz	15 ml	1

TEMPERATURE

FARENHEIT	CELSIUS
100 °F	37 °C
150 °F	65 °C
200 °F	93 °C
250 °F	121 °C
300 °F	150 °C
325 °F	160 °C
350 °F	180 °C
375 °F	190 °C
400 °F	200 °C
425 °F	220 °C
450 °F	230 °C
500 °F	260 °C
525 °F	274 °C
550 °F	288 °C

BONUS: 30 Days Meal Plan

Week 1

Day 1

Breakfast: French Omelet

Lunch: Chicken Caesar Salad

Dinner: Baked Ziti

Day 2

Breakfast: Quinoa and Peanut Butter

Lunch: Lentil Soup

Dinner: Beef Stroganoff

Day 3

Breakfast: Bacon, Potato, and Kale Frittata

Lunch: Gluten-Free Greek Salad

Dinner: Tacos

Day 4

Breakfast: Gluten-Free Banana Bread

Lunch: Stir-Fry with Chicken

Dinner: Chicken Pot Pie

Day 5

Breakfast: Breakfast Salad with Avocado and Eggs

Lunch: Vegetable Curry

Dinner: Fried Rice

Day 6

Breakfast: Cassava Pancakes

Lunch: Gluten-Free Broccoli Salad

Dinner: Shepherd's Pie

Day 7

Breakfast: Egg Bites Inspired

Lunch: Gluten-Free Minestrone Soup

Dinner: Lasagna

Week 2

Day 8

Breakfast: Zucchini Muffins with Greek Yogurt Icing

Lunch: Gluten-Free Taco Salad

Dinner: Gluten-Free Meatballs

Day 9

Breakfast: Chocolate Chip Cookies

Lunch: Tomato Soup

Dinner: Baked Salmon

Day 10

Breakfast: Gluten-Free Pancakes

Lunch: Spinach and Feta Stuffed Sweet Potatoes

Dinner: Gluten-Free Pizza

Day 11

Breakfast: Lemon Pound Cake

Lunch: Gluten-Free Caprese Salad

Dinner: Chicken prepared on a grill

Day 12

Breakfast: Quinoa Salad

Lunch: Zucchini Noodle Stir-Fry

Dinner: Gluten-Free Pasta

Day 13

Breakfast: Cake Donuts

Lunch: Gluten-Free Waldorf Salad

Dinner: Red Velvet Cake

Day 14

Breakfast: Buttermilk Biscuits with Sausage Gravy

Lunch: Gluten-Free Bread

Dinner: Vegetable Curry

Week 3

Day 15

Breakfast: Quinoa and Peanut Butter

Lunch: Lentil Soup

Dinner: Beef Stroganoff

Day 16

Breakfast: French Omelet

Lunch: Gluten-Free Greek Salad

Dinner: Tacos

Day 17

Breakfast: Bacon, Potato, and Kale Frittata

Lunch: Vegetable Curry

Dinner: Fried Rice

Day 18

Breakfast: Gluten-Free Banana Bread

Lunch: Chicken Caesar Salad

Dinner: Lasagna

Day 19

Breakfast: Breakfast Salad with Avocado and Eggs

Lunch: Stir-Fry with Chicken

Dinner: Chicken Pot Pie

Day 20

Breakfast: Cassava Pancakes

Lunch: Gluten-Free Broccoli Salad

Dinner: Shepherd's Pie

Day 21

Breakfast: Egg Bites Inspired

Lunch: Gluten-Free Minestrone Soup

Dinner: Baked Ziti

Week 4

Day 22

Breakfast: Chocolate Chip Cookies

Lunch: Tomato Soup

Dinner: Baked Salmon

Day 23

Breakfast: Gluten-Free Pancakes

Lunch: Spinach and Feta Stuffed Sweet Potatoes

Dinner: Gluten-Free Pizza

Day 24

Breakfast: Lemon Pound Cake

Lunch: Gluten-Free Caprese Salad

Dinner: Chicken prepared on a grill

Day 25

Breakfast: Quinoa Salad

Lunch: Zucchini Noodle Stir-Fry

Dinner: Gluten-Free Pasta

Day 26

Breakfast: Cake Donuts

Lunch: Gluten-Free Waldorf Salad

Dinner: Red Velvet Cake

Day 27

Breakfast: Gluten-Free Granola with Yogurt and Berries

Lunch: Gluten-Free Meatballs

Dinner: Vegetable Curry

Day 28

Breakfast: Gluten-Free Banana Bread

Lunch: Gluten-Free Bread

Dinner: Chicken Pot Pie

Made in United States
North Haven, CT
17 June 2023

37871630R00063